Other Books From Launch Point Press in the
Poetry for the New Millennium Series

By Sandra de Helen

The World's a Stage:
Life in Five Acts (2021)

Poetry for the People:
Heavy Verse (2020)

Lesbian Humor is Not an Oxymoron:
Light Verse (2019)

Desire Returns for a Visit:
Intimate Poems about Lesbian Love (2018)

I Eat My Words

Poetry and Recipes

By
Sandra de Helen

2022

A Launch Point Press Trade Paperback Original
I Eat My Words is a work of poetic fiction. Names, characters, places, and incidents are either the product of the author's imagination or are used fictitiously. Any resemblance to actual persons living or dead, business establishments, events, or locales is entirely coincidental.

Copyright © 2022 by Sandra de Helen

All rights reserved. Launch Point Press supports copyright which enables creativity, free speech, and fairness. Thank you for buying the authorized version of this book and for following copyright laws by not using or reproducing any part of this book in any manner whatsoever, including Internet usage, without written permission from Launch Point Press, except in the form of brief quotations embodied in critical reviews and articles. Your cooperation and respect supports authors and allows Launch Point Press to continue to publish the books you want to read.

ISBN: 978-1-63304-231-5
Ebook: 978-1-63304-108-0

FIRST EDITION: First Printing, 2022

Editing: Lori L. Lake
Copyediting/Proofreading: Sarah Rohrs
Book and Cover Design: Lorelei

Portland, Oregon
www.LaunchPointPress.com

Table of Contents

Author's Foreword
Dedication

Intro

1 ✒ Ode to Frost-free Refrigerators

Soups

5 ✒ Stormy's Soups
6   Stormy's Potato Soup
7   Stormy's Celery Soup
9   Stormy's Veggie Soup

Salads

13   Greek Orzo Salad
15   Pasta Salad: Red Peppers, Artichoke Hearts, and Cheese
17 ✒ Why Though?
19   Quinoa Mango Salad
21 ✒ Sweet and Spicy
22   Fruit Salad with a Kick

Breads, Sauces & Gravy

25 ✒ Ode to Biscuits
26 ✒ Yogurt Biscuits, Light and Fluffy

27 Yogurt Biscuits

29 Gravy with My Biscuits

30 Nutritional Yeast Gravy

31 Mushroom Marsala Sauce

32 Mushroom Marsala Sauce (Vegetarian)

Vegetable Dishes

37 Roasted Artichokes

39 Okra, My Love

40 Crispy Fried Okra (Bhindi)

Entrees

45 Making a Soufflé

47 Julia Child's Cheese Soufflé

51 Ode to Plant-based Meatloaf

52 Plant-based Meatloaf Recipe

53 Stormy's Lentil Loaf

55 A Fettucine Day

56 Fettucine with Marinated Artichoke Hearts

58 Impossible Burger Chili

59 Quiche in a Skillet

60 Skillet Quiche

61 ✒ Comfort Foods (Mac and Cheese)
62   Stovetop Macaroni and Cheese
64   My Homemade Veggie Pot Pie

Desserts

69 ✒ German Chocolate Cake
71   German's Chocolate Cake

77 ✒ Chocolate Days, Chocolate Nights
78   Sandra's Favorite Chocolate Cake
80   Chocolate Buttercream Frosting

81 ✒ Easy as Pie
82   Chocolate Mousse Pie

83 ✒ Mom's Cream Puffs
84   Cream Puffs

86 ✒ Give Me a Lime
87   Lime-Glazed Pound Cake

90 ✒ Tangerine

92 ✒ Olive Oil Cake
93   Mandarin Orange Olive Oil Cake
97   Gluten-Free Fudgy Chocolate Cake

97 ✒ Mom's Only Cake
98   Pineapple Upside Down Cake

100 Coconut Cake, My Favorite
101   Coconut Cake (simple)
103   Raspberry Coconut Cake (advanced)

107 Secret Ingredient
108   Aunt Inez's Ole Southern Butter Cake & Sauce

110 Joy of Cheesecake
111   Joy of Cooking New York Cheesecake

Outro

117 When the Cupboard Contains Only Onions and Olive Oil

Afterword

About The Author

Acknowledgments

Appendix – Cooking/Baking Conversion Charts

Foreword

Before I learned to eat my words, I often ate cake instead. Now I realize I can do both. I've reflected on my life and found I often said things that hurt people, usually the people I love most. I'm sure I still do on occasion, but I try hard not to hurt anyone with my words now.

No matter where you are in your journey, you have to eat. Why not eat cake? And roasted artichokes, or delicious soup? While you're cooking or baking, you can think loving thoughts of those who will partake of your offerings.

Love is the not-so-secret ingredient in all of our best meals. With this book, I share my favorite recipes with you. Each one is a favorite, some my own creations, some my daughter's, my mother's, my grandma's, or my aunt's.

Sandra de Helen
Portland, Oregon
June 2022

To the best cook in our family
and the light of my life,
my daughter Stormy.

Intro

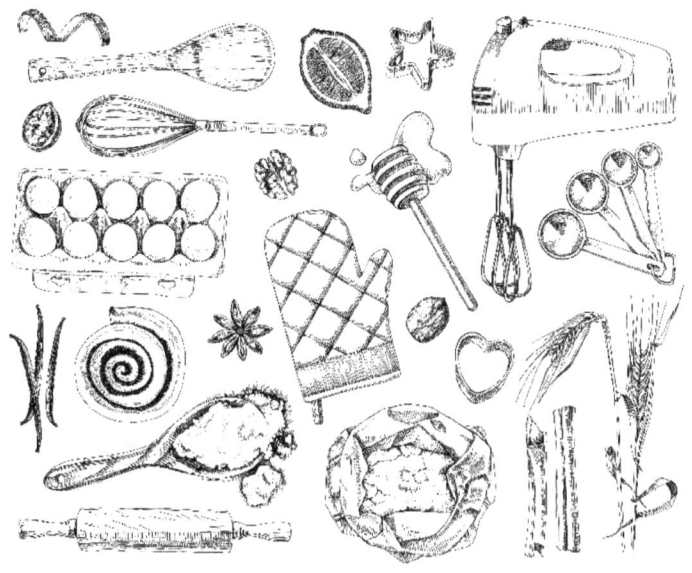

Please Note

There is an appendix at the back of this book that contains information about cooking and baking measurements and conversions from US to Metric.

Ode to Frost-free Refrigerators
(while defrosting, make Stormy's Potato Soup)

Before we had electricity, we had no fridge.
In the country, we used the earth
to cool our produce.

Cellars. Potatoes, onions, apples
and home-canned fruit and veggies
lined the shelves.

Eggs were fresh, and used daily.
Butter was churned by hand.
Milk came from the cow.

When we finally got a refrigerator
it seemed like a miracle.
Cold milk! Store bought cheese.

But frost would build up
in the tiny freezer. Then
came defrosting day.

Contents piled on the counter
rags and mops at the ready,
waiting for the frost to fall.

We've been frost-free for decades,
always have ice and ice cream,
frozen fruit and veggies.

We take this miracle for granted
now. I don't miss the days
of defrosting.

I celebrate the beauty
of the frost-free refrigerator.
Thank you, Westinghouse.

Soups

Stormy's Soups

Nothing is more healing
or more comforting

than great tasting soup.
Stormy makes the best

potato soup, celery soup,
every soup she makes is sublime.

She was born to cook
and started when she was eight.

Like all great chefs, she knows
what to add, what to subtract.

Her potato soup is creamy
without adding cream.

Her celery soup tastes like
fresh celery out of the garden,

without the strings. With butter
and few other ingredients,

Stormy's soups sing to my soul
and make my body happy.

Stormy's Potato Soup

Ingredients:
- 5-6 large potatoes, cut into small pieces
- 1-2 onions, chopped
- 2-3 stalks celery, chopped
- 1/2 stick butter
- salt
- pepper
- rosemary
- Veggie broth
- 1/2 cup to 1 cup milk

Directions:
1. Sauté onions in the butter over med low heat.
2. When the onions are translucent, add potatoes and celery.
3. Add salt and pepper. Fry until softened. Don't burn them. (Frying enhances flavor.)
4. Add enough broth to cover by no more than 1/2 inch. Add lid to pot and cook until potatoes are soft.
5. Use a stick blender (or old-fashioned egg beater) to blend the soup.
6. Add rosemary and more pepper.
7. Add 1/2 cup to 1 cup milk, allow it to heat. Serve hot.

Don't slurp your soup.
Unless you can't help yourself.

Stormy's Celery Soup

Ingredients:
- 2 full stalks of celery, including leaves
- 1 yellow onion
- 1/2 stick butter
- 1 small potato
- 1 quart veggie broth
- 1 cup milk
- salt and pepper to taste

Directions:
1. Chop all veggies.

2. Melt butter in a heavy bottom pot large enough to make your soup.

3. Add chopped onions and sauté on low until translucent (about 5 mins)

4. Add chopped potato.

5. Add chopped celery.

6. Sauté everything in the pot for another 5-10 mins on low heat.

7. Add broth.

8. Add salt and pepper to taste.

9. Cover and cook on low heat until tender.

10. Blend using an immersion (stick) blender (or transfer in smaller amounts to a regular blender and blend each amount until all is smooth).

11. Stir in 1 cup milk and taste.

12. Add Salt and Pepper if needed.

Go green!

Stormy's Veggie Soup

Ingredients and Directions:

1. In soup pot, over medium-high heat, heat 2 Tbsp of olive oil.

2. Add 1 chopped onion and some garlic, to taste.

3. Cook and stir until translucent . . . about 5 minutes.

4. Add chopped veggies:

- a few potatoes
- plenty of carrots
- 6-8 sticks of celery (or more if you love celery)
- cauliflower
- broccoli
- bok choy
- brussels sprouts
- sweet potato
- napa cabbage
- green cabbage
- green beans
- lima beans

Or add whatever you love and/or have on hand.

STUFF THE POT FULL OF VEGGIES!

5. Add a can of lite coconut milk.

6. Add a quart of organic chicken broth (vegan version: use veggie broth, or water.

7. Salt and pepper to taste (about 1-1/2 tsp of coarse salt and 1 tsp coarse ground black pepper).

8. Cook over medium low heat until the potatoes and carrots are done.

9. (Optional): Add fresh cilantro or ground coriander.

10. Serve hot.

Soup is a great way to get more veggies!

Salads

Greek Orzo Salad

Ingredients:
For the Greek Vinaigrette:
- 2 cloves garlic, minced
- 1/2 tsp dried basil
- 1/2 tsp oregano
- 1/2 tsp salt
- 1/2 tsp pepper
- 1/2 tsp Dijon mustard
- 1/2 cup red wine vinegar
- 3 Tbsps lemon juice
- 1/2 cup olive oil

For the Salad:
- 1 pound dried orzo cooked according to package directions
- 2 cups cucumber, cut into quarter-moons
- 2 cups chopped tomatoes or sliced cherry tomatoes
- 1/2 cup chopped red onion
- 1/4 cup minced fresh dill
- 1/3 cup sliced Kalamata olives (optional)

Directions for the Vinaigrette:
1. Mix together the garlic, herbs, salt, pepper and mustard in a medium-size glass.

2. Slowly whisk in the vinegar, lemon juice, and oil, then set that aside.

Directions for the Salad:

1. In a large bowl with a lid, mix together the orzo, cucumber, tomatoes, onion, dill, and olives.

2. Pour in about two thirds of the vinaigrette, and then stick all that in the fridge to chill for at least thirty minutes or up to overnight.

3. Before you're ready to serve, stir up the salad, taste, and add more of the dressing if you're into it.

Note: You can add 1-1/2 cups cooked chickpeas to this orzo salad for protein.

A balanced diet helps you feel your best. Veggies, protein, and cake are essential. At least at my house.

Pasta Salad: Red Peppers, Artichoke Hearts, and Cheese

Ingredients:
For the dressing:
- 1/2 cup Greek yogurt
- 1/4 cup olive oil
- minced garlic to taste
- 2 Tbsp of your preferred vinegar (I use a Korean black vinegar)
- 1 Tbsp Sriracha sauce (more if you like it spicier)
- 2 tsps honey
- 1 tsp pink mineral salt (or your favorite large-grained salt)
- Freshly ground black pepper

For the pasta salad:
- 1 pound (16 ounces) penne pasta, cooked al dente
- 1 (12-ounce) jar of fire-roasted red peppers, rinsed and chopped (1 heaping cup)
- 10-12 ounces cheese. I've tried crumbled feta, cubed smoked gouda, or shredded sharp white cheddar.
- 1/2 cup artichoke hearts, rinsed and chopped. This is about 6 ounces. Trader Joe's has 12-ounce jars.

Directions:
1. Cook the noodles according to package directions.
2. Drain, shaking to remove excess water.
3. Drizzle with a few Tbsps of olive oil and toss to coat.

For the dressing:
1. Combine Greek yogurt, olive oil, garlic, vinegar, sriracha sauce, honey, and salt in a small bowl, and whisk thoroughly.
2. Season generously with black pepper.

For the pasta salad:
1. Toss the cooked noodles, peppers, artichokes, and cheese together in a large bowl.
2. Pour the dressing over the top and mix to combine.
3. Taste and adjust any seasonings, if necessary.
4. Allow to rest at room temperature for 30 minutes before serving—or cover and refrigerate overnight. (Allow thirty minutes to warm to room temperature before serving).

This salad is guaranteed to impress your guests.

Why Though?

My favorite letter is querulous,
questioning, and queer.
It gives me quarters, quenches
my thirst, queries publishers,
and includes me in quartets.

Quiet and quick to support
this letter understands the need
for companionship. Seldom seen
without its friend, the little u.

Q provides its quota of grains
with quinoa and Quaker oats.
Quiche, quark, queso, and
quesadilla serve cheesy goodness.

For non-vegetarians, quail
and quahog clams give protein.

Quince is a fruit from a flowering
tree native to Iran and Turkey.

I'm never in a quagmire when
playing scrabble with my favorite
letter Q. I have no qualms

about using qadi, qats, qaid,
qoph, or even qi in order to collect
those extra Q points.

Quinoa Mango Salad

Ingredients:
For the Salad:
- 1 cup quinoa
- 2 cups cold water
- 1/4 tsp salt
- 1/4 cup blanched slivered or sliced almonds
- 2 Tbsp roasted pumpkin seeds
- 1 medium cucumber, peeled and diced
- 1 ripe mango, peeled and chopped
  OR: 1/2 cup dried mango slices, soaked overnight, then cut in 1/2-inch cubes

For the Dressing:
- 2 Tbsp olive oil
- 1/4 tsp turmeric
- Juice of 1 lime
- 2 Tbsp chopped fresh cilantro
- Salt and freshly ground black pepper

Directions for the Salad:
1. Wash quinoa and boil in water for ten minutes. Cover and let quinoa sit until it absorbs all the water. Fluff quinoa with a fork and let it cool to room temperature.
2. Peel the mango and cut into cubes.

3. Peel and slice the cucumber thinly.

4. Add cucumber to mango along with the almonds and pumpkin seeds.

5. Add the cooled quinoa to the mango mixture, pour the dressing over the salad, and toss.

Directions for the Dressing:
1. Heat turmeric in 1 tsp oil in a small pan on med-low for thirty to sixty seconds, then set aside to cool.

2. Add the lime juice to the oil & turmeric.

3. Mix in olive oil, cilantro, salt and pepper with a whisk or a fork.

4. Serve immediately or cover and chill for later.

Or Netflix and chill later, whatever. (Netflix and chill means making out, having sex, etc. ☺)

Sweet and Spicy

The first time I saw fruit salad
it delighted my eyes.
But it didn't taste right.

Apples, oranges, and bananas
covered in thick, white mayo
all topped with maraschino cherries.

Versions of this salad appeared
at Thanksgiving dinners, potlucks,
and cafeterias everywhere.

Then I made my own.
My version has evolved over the years
to suit my own need for sweet and spicy.

Mangos, banana, and berries
both red and black are tossed
with a lighter dressing.

Yogurt with maple syrup and a kick
of lime juice. Then to top it off
I add a healthy dash of chili powder.

My taste buds sparkle and sing
with joy to meet this mix of bite
and heat.

Fruit Salad with a Kick

Ingredients:
Fruit:
- 2 mangos
- 1 banana
- 1 cup strawberries
- 1 cup blackberries

Dressing:
- 1 cup plain yogurt
- 2 Tbsps maple syrup
- 2 Tbsps lime juice
- 1 Tbsp Chili powder

Directions:
1. Cut up mango, banana, and strawberries. Blackberries can be left whole.
2. Combine yogurt, maple syrup, and lime juice.
3. Pour mixture over fruit.
4. Sprinkle with Chili powder.

Take pictures of your beautiful salad!

Breads, Sauces & Gravy

Ode to Biscuits

Grandma made biscuits
every morning for breakfast.

Mom popped hers from a can
bought at Blue's Market.

My favorite biscuits to bake
are made from my favorite food.

Yogurt biscuits, so light
they nearly float away.

Made without processors
or mixers or any noise

other than my own hands
cutting in the butter,

kneading and pressing
the dough into shape.

I can make these while
the house sleeps,

Have them hot and ready
when it's time to break fast.

Yogurt Biscuits, Light and Fluffy

A long-time favorite of mine
I once decided to prepare them
for my friends in Dublin.

I didn't have my cookbook
and I hadn't copied the recipe
to my laptop.

Instead I searched my friend's
cookbook library for a recipe.
And found one.

Her husband made a pot of soup,
I provided the bread.
Her recipe was not quite the same

as the one I used, but when in Rome . . .
The soup was hearty and delicious
the yogurt biscuits were sweet and crunchy.

Because in some parts of the world
biscuits are what I call cookies.

Yogurt Biscuits

Ingredients:
- 3 cups all-purpose flour
- 1-1/4 tsp salt
- 4-1/2 tsp baking powder
- 1-1/2 tsp baking soda
- 8 Tbsp. cold, unsalted butter, cut into 8 to 10 pieces
- 1-1/4 cups plain yogurt

Directions:
1. Preheat the oven to 450°F.

2. In a large bowl, mix together the dry ingredients. Using your fingers, cut the butter into the dry ingredients until the entire mixture resembles coarse cornmeal.

3. Stir the yogurt into the dry ingredients with a spoon, until the mixture comes together. If some of the dry ingredients are still loose at the bottom of the bowl, stir in an additional spoonful of yogurt, then with your hands press all the dough together into a shaggy ball.

4. Turn the dough out onto a lightly floured surface and knead several times, until the dough is holding together. (Don't worry if it's a little sticky.) On the floured surface, press dough into a 3/4-inch-thick rectangle and cut into biscuits with a round glass or biscuit cutter dipped into flour.

5. Place the biscuits onto an ungreased baking sheet. Reshape the leftover dough, being careful not to overwork it, and cut out more biscuits.

6. Bake for eight to ten minutes, until the biscuits are golden-brown. These biscuits are best served warm.

And don't call these biscuits "cookies," whatever you do.

Gravy with My Biscuits

I'm a country girl. I love gravy.
Growing up, it was milk gravy

made with bacon grease.
Or brown gravy from the roast.

But I grew into a city girl,
a vegetarian, a healthy eater.

Yogurt biscuits made me happy,
but where was the gravy?

My daughter introduced me
to nutritional yeast gravy.

It's better than the gravies
of my country youth.

The yellow color is sunshine
on the lips. The yeasty taste

provides the promised
nutrition and vitamins.

Best of all, it covers my biscuits
in creamy goodness.

Nutritional Yeast Gravy

Ingredients:
- 1/4 cup flour
- 1/2 cup nutritional yeast
- 1/3 cup oil (safflower or other veggie oil)
- 2 to 2-1/2 cups of liquid (veggie stock, broth, or water)
- 1/4 to 1/3 cup Tamari sauce (or soy sauce)
- Cayenne pepper
- Paprika

Directions:

1. First, toast 1/4 cup flour and 1/2 cup nutritional yeast in a skillet/frying pan. Then transfer to a smaller, higher-sided saucepan. (You don't have to, but it's better—if you're willing to wash another dish.)

2. Add 1/3 cup oil (safflower or other veg oil).

3. Start whisking! Add, slowly, 2 to 2-1/2 cups liquid, either veggie stock or water (preferably heated). Whisk fast!

4. Sprinkle some cayenne and paprika to taste.

5. Add 1/4 to 1/3 cup tamari (or soy sauce) to taste. Whisk!

Pour this gravy on a biscuit or two. Or on mashed potatoes. Yum!

Mushroom Marsala Sauce

If you like mushrooms, you'll love
mushroom marsala sauce.
Ask my sister.

Creamy, comforting, and versatile
you can cover noodles or rice
or scoop it over a lentil loaf.

There is a non-alcoholic version
if you don't consume marsala wine.
Easy to make, even in double batches.

In the time of Covid, I revisit
in memory the lesbian potlucks of my youth
when Candice brought her honey cheesecake,

Paula's table was laden with green and pasta salads,
Kate's hearty crock of thirteen bean soup,
Lois and Joanie's casseroles with melted cheese.

I would love to bring homemade noodles
and a pot of warm mushroom marsala sauce
to share with every woman I've ever loved.

Laughter would once again warm the air
as we breathed each other's love
into our healthy lungs.

Mushroom Marsala Sauce (Vegetarian)

Ingredients:
- 1/3 cup butter
- 2 tsps minced shallots or green onions
- 2 tsps minced garlic (more or less, I use less)
- 8 ounces of fresh, sliced mushrooms
- 1/4 cup marsala wine *(or you can substitute:* **Non-Alcohol Marsala Substitute***: 1/4 cup of white grape juice, 1 Tbsp vanilla extract, 2 Tbsps of sherry vinegar. Mix in 1/4 cup in the recipe.)*
- 1/4 tsp ground black pepper
- 1 cup vegetable stock,
- 2 tsps potato starch, or flour
- 1 tsp minced fresh parsley
- 2 Tbsps heavy cream
- 4 servings of cooked pasta (linguini)

Directions:

1. Melt butter over low heat in a medium saucepan.

2. Turn heat up to medium/high to sauté the shallots and garlic for about thirty seconds (be careful not to burn the butter). Add Marsala wine, simmer for another thirty seconds or so, then add mushrooms and black pepper. Simmer over medium/high heat for five minutes.

3. Dissolve potato starch in vegetable stock. Add stock to the saucepan and simmer for an additional five minutes.

4. Add parsley and cream to the sauce and simmer for three to four minutes or until thick. Remove pan from the heat, then cover it until needed.

5. Pour sauce over the cooked linguini and toss to coat.

Preparation Tips: Many of the ingredients need to be added fairly quickly so measure everything out ahead of time and have it ready. If you start the pasta water first, then start the sauce, the pasta will be ready about the same time as the sauce. (Just put the water on the burner, turn it to boil and start working on the sauce. It's easy to take ten seconds to toss the pasta in once the water comes to a boil.)Use the five minutes that the mushrooms are simmering to dissolve the cornstarch and mince the parsley (have it rinsed and ready beforehand).

If you're a wine drinker, you can sip a glass of Marsala as you prepare this dish.
I'm not, so I just sniff the bottle.

Vegetable Dishes

Roasted Artichokes

<u>Ingredients</u>:
For the artichokes:
- 3 large artichokes
- 3 tsp lemon juice
- salt and pepper
- extra virgin olive oil
- 6 garlic cloves
- 1 small shallot, thinly sliced
- 1 Tbsp capers
- crumbled feta cheese (for final step)

For the vinaigrette:
- Same 6 garlic cloves, roasted earlier with the artichokes
- 1/2 cup chopped fresh dill
- 1/4 cup fresh lemon juice
- 1 tsp honey
- salt and pepper

Directions:
1. Pre-heat oven to 400°F.

2. To clean artichokes, first, cut off the stem/stalk. Peel off the tough outer layers by hand. When you reach the softer layers, use a serrated knife to cut off about 3/4 inches from the top. Now, cut artichoke in half, length-

wise. Then, using a spoon, remove the fuzzy choke on the inside of the artichoke.

3. As you clean the inside of each artichoke half, immediately add 1/2 tsp lemon juice to cover the surface to prevent the artichoke from discoloring.

4. On a large baking sheet, place each artichoke half in a piece of lightly-oiled foil paper that is large enough to fold around.

5. Season artichokes with salt and pepper, and nestle one garlic clove in the center of each artichoke half. Drizzle generously with quality olive oil (it's okay if some of the olive oil pools in the center or overflows onto the foil). Close the foil around artichokes.

6. Roast artichoke halves in the oven heated to 400°F for forty minutes.

7. Using tongs, carefully open the foil pouches. Remove the roasted garlic from the center of artichoke, and close up the foil until ready to serve. Let garlic cool.

8. In small food processor bowl, add roasted garlic with the remaining vinaigrette ingredients. Pulse 'til smooth.

9. Remove artichokes from foil. Arrange on a serving platter, generously drizzle the roasted garlic-dill vinaigrette. Top with shallots, capers. and crumbled feta cheese.

Enjoy!

Okra, My Love

How can you love okra? they ask.
Many seem baffled by this charming
vegetable because it oozes slime.

Fuzzy ribbed tubes of jade, Kelly, and
fern green, shaped like lanterns, their ends
capped and tipped, okra grows like green beans,
but tastes like spring.

At first, I knew okra only from cans.
Mom was not a cook. But when she
rolled the sliced rounds in corn meal
and fried them in bacon grease, yum.

Next, I had fresh okra cooked
with tomatoes at an Indian restaurant
in Iowa City. A kind of stew,
called bhindi masala.

My favorite method is also called bhindi,
or crispy fried okra. It has lots of spice,
and makes a perfect side dish, adding
beauty, interest, and deliciousness
to your meal.

Crispy Fried Okra (Bhindi)

Ingredients

- 12 ounces fresh or frozen baby okra bhindi, thawed if using frozen
- 3 Tbsps fat of choice ghee, or avocado oil
- 1/2 tsp cumin seeds
- 1 onion diced
- 1 Serrano pepper
- 2 cloves garlic minced
- 1/2-inch ginger, minced
- 1/4 tsp turmeric
- 1/4 tsp salt adjust to taste

Directions

1. Rinse okra, and slice into rounds. Spread them out onto a paper towel to dry while you prep the remaining ingredients. The okra must be completely dry.

2. Melt 2 Tbsps of fat in a sauté pan over medium-high heat.

3. Add cumin seeds and once they begin to brown or splutter, add the onions and serrano pepper.

4. Sauté for ten minutes, or until the onions begin to brown. Then add the garlic, ginger, and spices and mix well.

5. Reduce heat to medium and add the remaining one Tbsp of fat and the okra. Stir-fry for ten to twelve minutes or until the okra is dry and crispy.

You might convert a non-okra lover with this recipe.

Entrees

Making a Soufflé

The recipe is simple enough.
The execution is not.

I am adventurous.
I bought a soufflé dish.

I bought Julie Child's cookbook.
I made her cheese soufflé,

but only for myself. Just in case.
Soufflés are notorious

for falling. I used to fall myself,
not over, but over and over

in love with the wrong sorts.
I would puff up with love,

Then deflate in hurt feelings,
jealousy, or disillusionment.

Soufflés want their eggs beaten
hard, but folded softly.

They don't like sudden cold,
you must not open the oven door.

I am not as fragile as a soufflé,
but I too want to be treated

properly. With respect for my needs.
Sudden cold can fell me in my tracks.

I heeded every instruction Julia gave,
my cheese soufflé was beautiful,

and delicious. I no longer fall in love,
and I respect my own needs.

Julia Child's Cheese Soufflé

Ingredients
- 3 Tbsp of butter plus 1 Tbsp for buttering the mold
- 1 Tbsp grated Gruyere cheese for dusting the mold
- 3 Tbsp flour
- 1 cup milk lightly boiling
- 4 egg yolks
- 5 egg whites
- 1 cup grated Gruyere cheese
- 1/2 tsp cayenne or paprika
- Salt and pepper to taste
- Pinch of nutmeg
- 1/4 tsp cream of tartar for the egg whites

Directions

1. Preheat oven to 400°F.

2. Start by buttering the mold and sprinkling with cheese.

3. The foil wrap: This will make sure that your soufflé will not spill over and will keep a high mold. Tear a piece of foil so that it is long enough to wrap around your mold. Fold in half length-wise and butter one side. The buttered side will be the "inside" of the mold.

4. Wrap the foil around the mold. Secure loose top ends with metal paper clips.

5. Melt the 3 Tbsp of butter in a sauce pan and stir in the flour with a spatula, cooking over medium heat until the butter and flour foam together for about two minutes without browning.

6. Remove from heat. When mixture has stopped bubbling, pour in all of the boiling milk at once and beat vigorously with a whisk until well blended.

7. Beat in the seasonings, cayenne or paprika, nutmeg and salt and pepper. Return to moderate heat and continue to stir with a whisk for another minute. The mixture will be very thick.

8. Remove from heat, take the egg yolks and beat one egg yolk into your white cream mixture one at a time until well incorporated.

9. Now for the egg whites. In a clean, dry mixing bowl, begin to beat your egg whites with a whisk attachment on low speed. You will see that the egg whites will "break up" and begin to have a foamy consistency.

10. As the egg whites are foaming, increase the speed gradually and add cream of tartar and a pinch of salt. Increase the speed to fast and continue to beat for a few more minutes.

11. If you're using a stand mixer, do not turn away from your egg whites! Continue checking them. What you want to see are "traces" on the surface. The egg whites should also have a glossy white sheen and be able to be stiff and firm when holding with a whisk.

12. Once the egg whites are done, don't let them sit for long. Take a large spoonful and stir it into the cream mixture to lighten it.

13. Stir in all but about 1 Tbsp of the grated cheese into the cream mixture.

14. There is a technique to folding the rest of the egg whites. Take one large spoonful of the egg whites and using your spatula, cut down the middle and draw the spatula under, while scraping the side of the pan and turning the pan with the other hand. Basically, you are folding under and to the side.

15. Continue with the rest of the egg whites. Be careful not to over fold. It's okay if there are white streaks leftover. Now your mixture is ready. Carefully pour your mixture into the prepared mold. It should be about 3/4 high. Tap the mold carefully to even it out and top with remaining 1 Tbsp of cheese.

16. Place on middle-back rack of pre-heated 400°F oven. Once in, immediately turn down to 375°F.

17. Bake for exactly thirty minutes and DO NOT, I repeat, DO NOT open the oven door ever during those thirty minutes.

18. The soufflé will have puffed up a few inches over the mold and will be a gorgeous golden brown on top. Insert a tester, if it comes out clean, it's done.

19. To serve: Use 2 spoons and lightly puncture the top of the soufflé. Don't scoop from the bottom, that will deflate it, just spoon vertically.

*Holler **Bon Appetit!** in a French accent, even if only to yourself.*

Ode to Plant-based Meatloaf

Working class cooks use everything
in the cabinet, everything in the fridge.

Suppers must be created every evening
after a hard day's work.

Meatloaf, mashed potatoes, a vegetable
and everyone gets filled up.

Leftover meatloaf makes sandwiches
to take to work and school.

Leftover mashed potatoes can be used
to create potato salad.

This vegetarian enjoyed only lentil loaf
until plant-based burger arrived.

Oh, Impossible Burger, you bring
the taste, the memories, the satisfaction.

I'm glad I lived long enough
to enjoy this delicious addition.

Plant-based Meatloaf Recipe

Ingredients:
- 12 ounces Impossible or Beyond Burger
- 1-1/2 cup barbecue sauce, divided
- 1/2 onion, chopped
- 1/2 red pepper, chopped
- 1/2 tsp garlic salt
- 1/2 tsp celery salt
- 1/2 tsp dry mustard
- 1/4 tsp cayenne
- 1/2 tsp paprika
- salt and pepper to taste

Directions:
1 Preheat oven to 400°F.

2 Prepare a loaf pan by spraying it with oil.

3. In a large bowl, mix 1 cup barbecue sauce with all other ingredients, using a fork or your hands. Turn into the loaf pan and bake for twenty-five mins.

4. Remove from oven and pour the remaining 1/2 cup barbecue sauce over top, spread it evenly, let rest fifteen to forty minutes before serving.

Even if you were never a meatloaf fan, you might enjoy this.

Stormy's Lentil Loaf

Ingredients:
- 2 cups water
- 1 tsp salt
- 1 cup lentils
- 1 small onion, diced
- 1 cup quick-cooking oats
- 1/2 cup pepper jack cheese, shredded
- 1 egg, beaten
- 1/2 cup red pepper sauce (homemade, or use Trader Joe's red pepper bruschetta)
- 1 tsp garlic powder
- 1 tsp dried basil
- 1 Tbsp dried parsley
- 1/2 tsp seasoning salt
- 1/2 tsp black pepper

Directions:

1. Add salt to water and boil in a saucepan.

2. Add lentils and simmer covered twenty-five to thirty minutes, until lentils are soft and most of water is evaporated.

3. Remove from heat and drain and partially mash lentils.

4. Scrape your mashed lentils into a mixing bowl and allow to cool slightly.

5. Stir in onion, oats and cheese until mixed.

6. Add egg, tomato sauce, garlic, basil, parsley, seasoning salt and pepper.

7. Mix well.

8. Spoon into loaf pan that has been generously sprayed with non-stick cooking spray, or well-greased. Smooth the top.

9. Bake at 350°F for thirty to forty-five minutes until firm.

10. Cool in pan on rack for ten minutes.

11. Run a knife around edges of pan, turn out loaf onto plate, and serve hot.

I live in Portland's Lents neighborhood where we call each other Lentils.

A Fettucine Day

Some days you just want to eat pasta.
You need the sunshine in your belly.

The light, long, thin strips of flour,
egg, and salt formed into beauty.

You want a sauce to give it life.
You love Trader Joe's artichoke hearts.

You keep your freezer stocked
with unsalted butter, and the cupboard

always holds pasta. You check
your supply of grated parmesan.

You have everything you need
to brighten your day.

Belly full, you contemplate
writing your list of five good things.

Fettucine with Marinated Artichoke Hearts

<u>Ingredients:</u>
- 12-ounce jar marinated artichokes
- Fettucine (fresh or packaged)
- 6 Tbsps unsalted butter, cubed, divided
- 1 tsp lemon zest
- 1/2 tsp freshly ground black pepper
- 4 ounces grated Parmesan cheese (about 1 cup), divided
- 1/4 tsp kosher salt, plus more salt for water

Directions:

1. Bring 6 quarts of salted water to a boil over high, add salt.

2. Drain artichokes; reserve 1 Tbsp marinade. Roughly chop artichokes; set aside.

3. Cook fettuccine in boiling water, stirring occasionally, until just tender and floating. Reserve one and a half cups of the cooking water in a heatproof measuring cup or bowl. Drain fettuccine; set aside.

4. Melt 4 Tbsps butter in a large nonstick skillet over medium-high until sizzling. Stir in chopped artichokes and reserved marinade.

5. Spread artichokes in an even layer and cook, undisturbed, six to eight minutes.

6. Stir in lemon zest, pepper, and 1-1/4 cups of the reserved cooking water. Bring to a simmer.

7. Add cooked fettuccine and remaining 2 Tbsps butter; toss with tongs to loosen fettuccine. Reduce heat to low.

8. Add 1/2 cup cheese, stirring and tossing until melted, about thirty seconds.

9. Add salt and remaining 1/2 cup cheese; cook, stirring and tossing, until sauce is silky and coats fettuccine, one to two minutes. Add remaining 1/4 cup cooking water if needed. Remove from heat. Serve immediately.

Personally, I like this way better than Fettucine Alfredo. Plus it has a vegetable!

Impossible Burger Chili

<u>Ingredients</u>:
- 12 ounces Impossible Burger
- 1 medium onion, chopped
- 1 Tbsp olive oil
- 1 can diced tomatoes
- 1 can chili beans
- 6 Tbsp chili powder (more or less, to taste)
- 1 Tbsp cumin (more or less, to taste)
- 1 tsp salt
- 1 tsp black pepper

Directions:

1. Sauté onion in olive oil until transparent.

2. Add crumbled impossible burger and brown it.

3. Add all the rest of the ingredients, tasting as you go until the chili is spicy enough for your taste.

4. Cook until heated through, then serve.

This chili is impossible not to love.

Quiche in a Skillet

Mom gave me her cast iron pans
when she stopped cooking.
Not that she ever did, really.

The tiny one-egg skillet
is perfect for that one thing.
The big ten inch one

is family size. We used it
for bacon and eggs
throughout my childhood.

It's also good for cornbread
though Mom's was inedible.
At least by me.

For the past four decades
I've used the black and seasoned
instrument for making quiche.

No need for pastry, my recipe
is quick and easy, and a good way
to use up leftover brown rice.

Many people have enjoyed
my lazy way of making dinner.
Maybe me most of all.

Skillet Quiche

Ingredients:
- 2-3 Tbsps Butter
- 4-5 eggs
- 2 cups Rice, cooked
- 8 ounces Mushrooms, sliced
- 1 Onion, chopped
- 1 cup cheddar cheese, shredded
- 1/4 cup Parmesan, shredded or ground

Directions:

1. Melt butter in large cast iron skillet, careful not to burn it.

2. Add onions, stir over med heat until translucent.

3. Add mushrooms first, then rice, stir to combine.

4. Lower heat and add eggs, salt and pepper, and cheese (in that order)

5. Cook until fully set (insert clean table knife in middle to check), about ten to fifteen minutes.

6. Sprinkle top with Parmesan and serve.

Easier than making pastry, and so hearty!

Comfort Foods (Mac and Cheese)

The first time I heard "comfort foods"
I assumed they meant mac and cheese.

I was young and ignorant.
People everywhere have their version

of which foods comfort them.
Dal, pho, ramen noodles, poutine.

French onion soup, chilaquiles,
they all sound good to me.

Chicken soup, mashed potatoes,
biscuits and gravy. Milk toast.

All of those are probably better
for you when you're sick,

better than my first thought:
macaroni and delicious cheese.

Pasta has a good mouth feel,
cheese offers taste and texture,

the creaminess of the combo
fills your belly and inspires dreams.

If that isn't comfort,
I don't know what is.

Stovetop Macaroni and Cheese

Ingredients:
- 1-1/2 cups water
- 1 cup milk
- 8 ounces elbow macaroni
- 4 ounces white cheddar, shredded (1 cup)
- 4 ounces extra-sharp cheddar cheese, shredded (1 cup)
- 1/2 tsp Dijon mustard
- Small pinch cayenne pepper
- 1/2 cup panko bread crumbs
- 1 Tbsp. extra-virgin olive oil
- salt and pepper
- 2 Tbsp. grated Parmesan cheese

Directions:

1. Bring water and milk to boil in medium saucepan over high heat.

2. Stir in macaroni and reduce heat to medium-low. Cook, stirring frequently, until macaroni is soft (slightly past al dente), six-eight minutes. Do not drain any remaining moisture.

3. Add white cheddar cheese, mustard, and cayenne, and cook, stirring constantly, until cheese is completely melted, about a minute.

4. Off heat, stir in extra-sharp cheddar until evenly distributed but not melted. Cover saucepan and let stand for five minutes.

5. Meanwhile, combine panko, oil, 1/8 tsp salt, and 1/8 tsp pepper in 8-inch nonstick skillet until panko is evenly moistened.

6. Cook over medium heat, stirring frequently, until evenly browned, three to four minutes.

7. Off heat, sprinkle Parmesan over panko mixture and stir to combine. Transfer panko mixture to small bowl.

8. Stir macaroni until sauce is smooth (sauce may look loose but will thicken as it cools).

9. Season with salt and pepper to taste. Transfer to warm serving dish and sprinkle panko mixture over top. Serve immediately.

I didn't say it was quick, I said it was comforting. Make it and see!

My Homemade Veggie Pot Pie

Ingredients:
- 2 Tbsps olive oil
- 1 onion, chopped
- 8 ounces mushrooms, sliced
- 1 clove garlic, minced
- 2 large carrots, chopped
- 2 potatoes with peel, chopped
- 2 stalks celery, sliced
- 3 cups chopped fresh veggies (green beans, peas, broccoli, cauliflower, bok choy – your choice)
- 3 cups vegetable broth
- 1 tsp kosher salt
- 1 tsp ground black pepper
- 2 Tbsps potato starch
- 2 Tbsps Tamari
- 3 or 4 pre-premade pie crusts

Directions:
1 Preheat oven to 425°F.

2. Heat oil in a large skillet or saucepan. Cook onions, mushrooms, and garlic in oil for three to five minutes, stirring frequently.

3. Stir in carrots, potatoes, and celery. Stir in fresh veggies and vegetable broth. Bring to a boil, then turn heat down to a simmer.

4. Cook until vegetables are barely tender, about five minutes. Season with salt and pepper.

5. In a small bowl, mix the potato starch, Tamari, and 1/4 cup water until starch is completely dissolved. Stir into vegetables, and cook until sauce thickens, about three minutes.

6. Using your 3 or 4 pre-made pie crusts, roll out half of the dough to line the bottom of an 11x7-inch baking dish. (I use Trader Joe's pre-made pie crusts, or any dough recipe will work out fine.)

7. Pour the filling on top of the pastry crust lining the 11x7-inch pan.

8. Roll out the remaining pie crust dough, arrange over the filling, and seal and flute the edges to make one big pie.

9. Bake in preheated oven for thirty minutes, or until the crust is brown.

If you've always wanted to make your own pot pie, this is a good one.

Desserts

German Chocolate Cake

Why would a home baker attempt
a German chocolate cake?

The list of ingredients means
a trip to the store.

The instructions include
the cake, the filling, the icing.

Making this cake takes hours
and a clear mind for concentration.

Did you know that German chocolate
is named for a man, not a country?

Sam German created this chocolate
sweeter than semi-sweet in 1855.

In 1957, Mrs. George Clay of Texas
created the recipe for the cake.

Whoever Mrs. Clay was when she
was born remains a mystery.

Did she have a brother-in-law
with a sweet tooth? I do.

When she baked her special cake
who shared the deliciousness?

The pecans, the coconut, the custard?
The sweet chocolate sponge layers?

This is a cake for birthdays, anniversaries,
graduation, and other special days.

A good friend shared her special recipe
with me, and taught me to bake it

with love and patience, and a sprinkle
of pride.

German's Chocolate Cake
(with directions by Joanne Conger)

An American Classic cake based on a chocolate invented by an American man named German. There is nothing German about this cake except that American guy's name. [The original printed recipe appeared in the Dallas Morning Star newspaper in 1957, written by Mrs. George Clay. German's chocolate was created by Samuel German in 1852 and includes more sugar than the average semi-sweet chocolate.]

This is a complex cake so read through the directions and imagine, a little. With a baking skill level calculated from 1 to 10, this recipe is about a 7-8. OR—you just have to be really patient and do things one step at a time in the order noted. This cake is worth every moment of effort.

You will need a quality electric mixer to make this cake. It is a foam cake, so needs some hearty beating.

Prepare three round cake pans (8x2 or 9x2). Grease, line with wax paper, grease a little more (Do NOT flour the pans—no matter what anyone tells you.) I use disposable foil pans because they actually make a better cake.

Have all ingredients at room temperature (Room temperature if the room is fairly cool. Don't let your ingredients warm up too much.)

Ingredients:
For the Cake:
- 2-1/4 cups sifted cake flour (All-purpose is fine.)
- 1 tsp baking soda
- 1/2 tsp salt
- 4 ounces sweet baking chocolate fairly chopped
- 1/2 cup boiling water
- One tsp of quality vanilla
- 1 cup of buttermilk (sour cream will do—but, it's not better than buttermilk—and no "buttermilk substituting" allowed, either. Just get buttermilk.)
- 1 cup butter (2 sticks)
- 4 egg yolks
- 4 egg whites
- 1-3/4 cup sugar

For the Cake Foam
- 4 egg whites
- 1/4 tsp Cream of Tartar
- 1/4 cup sugar

For the Coconut Pecan Filling
- 2 cups of flaked coconut
- 2 cups of chopped pecans
- 1 cup sugar
- 1 cup heavy cream
- 3 large egg yolks
- 1/2 cup of butter cut into small pieces.

Directions for Making the Cake:

1. Preheat oven to 350°F. Convection oven 325°F.

2. Whisk together: 2-1/4 cups sifted cake flour (All-purpose is fine), 1 tsp baking soda, and 1/2 tsp salt.

3. Combine in a small bowl 4 ounces sweet baking chocolate fairly chopped and 1/2 boiling water

4. Stir until chocolate is melted and set aside. (Do this first—you don't want this mixture too warm.)

5. Stir in: 1 tsp of quality vanilla (Yes, high quality makes a difference.)

6. Have ready 1 cup of buttermilk (sour cream will do—but, it's not better than buttermilk—and no "buttermilk substituting" either. Just get buttermilk.)

7. Beat the buttermilk in a large bowl until light and fluffy—about four to six minutes:

8. Add 1 cup butter (2 sticks).

9. GRADUALLY add 1-3/4 cups sugar.

10. Beat in one at a time: 4 egg yolks (SAVE the whites—you will need them!)

11. On low speed, gradually add the melted chocolate and beat until JUST incorporated. You will need to be careful of overbeating. So, switch to hand mixing and finish with a few turns in the electric mixer. I hand mix a bit, then do a few electric mixer turns and then hand mix throughout the process.

13. While scraping the bowl of chocolate batter, mix in the set-aside buttermilk and the flour mixture in three parts.

Directions for Making the Cake Foam:
1. Beat the 4 egg whites & the 1/4 tsp of Cream of Tartar until fairly well mixed.

2. GRADUALLY add the 1/4 cup of sugar.
The peaks should be firm but fairly soft when done. They should peak with a softness that proves the whites are not dry. Dry whites would be a disaster—so do them over if you miss the mark.

3. Fold 1/3 of the whites into the batter with a spatula. Finish with about ten turns in the electric mixer. The batter should be fairly light.

4. Distribute the cake foam evenly in the three pans and spread out. Make sure the layers are about as even as possible.

5. Bake twenty-five to thirty minutes until the cake pulls away from the pan slightly. DO NOT OVERBAKE. It's better for this cake to be *just* barely done. Test with a toothpick.

6. Let cool for ten minutes and then turn out on a rack.

Directions for Making the Coconut Pecan Filling:

1. Toast 2 cups of flaked coconut and 2 cups of chopped pecan in the oven for about eight minutes (until brownish) and set aside to cool.

2. Combine in a medium saucepan:
   - 1 cup sugar
   - 1 cup heavy cream
   - 3 large egg yolks
   - 1/2 cup of butter but into small pieces. (Start cold. Not melted.)

3. Cook over medium heat stirring constantly until the mixture is thick and bubbling slightly. Cook for two or three minutes—stirring and stirring. Don't stop.

4. Remove from heat, let cool for about five minutes, and then add in the coconut and pecans. Divide into three parts.

5. Spread filling on top of layer one, then on layer two, and finally on the third layer—ONLY on the tops—do NOT ice the sides with anything.

Traditional German's Chocolate Cake is NAKED on the sides. And the cake is so sweet you simply do not need more frosting. Be a purist.

People who love German's chocolate cake are so grateful for this bake, it is totally worth the time and effort for you to make it for them. Especially if that person is you.

Chocolate Days, Chocolate Nights

Not every day is a chocolate day
for me. Most days I want salty
or citrus or the crunch of an apple.

I never ate chocolate until I made
hot cocoa in 4-H. I was eight years old.
It was okay.

Puberty brought on the cravings
for chocolate days, chocolate nights.
The smooth, silky feel of a chocolate bar
took away the sharp edge of pain.

Decades later, my cupboard contains
dark chocolate bars, truffles,
cocoa and semi-sweet chips for baking.

There is no shame in creating one's own
pain reliever in the shape of a lovely
chocolate cake with chocolate buttercream.

Sandra's Favorite Chocolate Cake

Ingredients:
- 2 cups all-purpose flour
- 2 cups sugar
- 3/4 cup unsweetened cocoa powder
- 2 teaspoons baking powder
- 1 1/2 teaspoons baking soda
- 1 teaspoon salt
- 1 1/2 teaspoon instant coffee
- 1 cup milk
- 1/2 cup melted coconut oil
- 2 large eggs
- 1 1/2 teaspoons vanilla extract
- 1 cup boiling water

Directions:

1. Preheat oven to 350º F. Prepare two 9-inch cake pans by spraying with baking spray (the kind with flour) or buttering and lightly flouring.

2. Add flour, sugar, cocoa, baking powder, baking soda, salt and instant coffee to the bowl of a stand mixer. Using the paddle attachment, stir on low until combined well.

3. Add milk, vegetable oil, eggs, and vanilla to flour mixture and mix together on medium speed until well combined.

4. Reduce speed and carefully add boiling water to the cake batter until well combined. The batter will be thin.

5. Distribute cake batter evenly between the two prepared cake pans. Bake for thirty to thirty-five minutes, until a toothpick or cake tester inserted in the center of the chocolate cake comes out clean.

6. Remove from the oven and allow to cool on a rack for about 10 minutes, remove from the pan and cool completely.

7. Frost cake with chocolate buttercream.

Remember: Moderation in all things. Except chocolate!

Chocolate Buttercream Frosting

Ingredients:
- 1 cup butter (two sticks)
- 3 ½ cups powdered sugar
- 1-1/2 cup cocoa powder
- 1 Tbsps milk
- 1 teaspoon salt (trust me, this makes all the difference)
- 1 teaspoon pure vanilla extract

Directions:

1. With stand mixer fitted with a paddle attachment, beat the butter on medium speed until creamy – about two minutes.
2. Add powdered sugar, cocoa powder, milk, salt, and vanilla extract.
3. Beat on low speed for thirty seconds, then increase to high speed and beat for a full minute. If the buttercream is too thin, add more powdered sugar; if too thick, add more milk, one tablespoon at a time. The frosting should be the color of milk chocolate and spread easily. If in doubt, spread it on a cracker first until you're satisfied with the consistency.
4. Use immediately or cover tightly and store for up to a week in the refrigerator.

That really tops the cake!

Easy as Pie

My hands don't like to be dirty.
They really don't care for sticky,
clinging pie dough.

When I do bake pies, I call
down Grandma Maggie's spirit
to help me face the process.

She taught me how to make pie crust
but not how to enjoy the hug
of wet patisserie.

Her own hugs were rarely bestowed
but always welcome. She smelled
of fresh peaches, honest sweat, and tobacco.

I would sacrifice five years of my life
to taste her peach cobbler once again.
I find little solace in my vegetarian pot pie.

Chocolate Mousse Pie

Ingredients:
- 2 cups semi-sweet chocolate chips
- 2 cups heavy cream (this is one pint)
- 2 tsps powdered sugar
- 1 tsp vanilla
- 1 nine-inch pre-baked pie shell (I use frozen ones from Trader Joe's)

Directions:

1. Add 3/4 cup heavy cream to the chocolate chips and microwave for a minute, then in fifteen second increments, stirring in between, until the mixture is smooth.

2. While the chocolate is cooling to room temperature, whip the remaining cream with powdered sugar and vanilla (in a chilled bowl) until soft peaks form.

3. Gently fold two cups of the whipped cream into the cooled chocolate mixture for the filling. When folding, turn your spoon or spatula in only one direction in order to maintain the fluffiness.

4. Spoon mixture into prepared pie crust.

5. Top with remaining whipped cream.

Be aware, chocolate lovers will want to lick their dishes when they're finished.

Mom's Cream Puffs

My mother didn't cook
because she didn't eat.

But somehow she learned
to bake cream puffs.

For her mother, she filled
them with sugar-free pudding.

I filled mine with whipped cream.
She didn't eat them.

When she died, she left behind
her simple recipe for cream puffs.

Otherwise known as *pâte à choux*,
or *choux* pastry, a fancy bake.

Not for Mom. It was simple,
whip them up, spoon them into

rounds, and bake them at 350.
When cool, slice open and fill.

Because she made it look easy,
I found them easy to make as well.

No piping bag necessary.
No need to speak French.

Cream Puffs

Ingredients:
- 3/4 cup water
- 3/4 cup whole milk
- 3/4 cup (1-1/2 sticks) unsalted butter, diced
- 1/2 tsp salt
- 1-1/2 cups sifted all-purpose flour (sifted, then measured)
- 6 large eggs, divided

Directions

1. Position one rack in top third and one rack in bottom third of oven and preheat to 425°F.

2. Line two large-rimmed baking sheets with parchment paper.

3. Bring first four ingredients to boil in heavy large saucepan over medium heat, stirring with wooden spoon until butter melts.

4. Add flour all at once and stir vigorously until dough forms and pulls away from sides of pan. Continue to stir until film forms on pan bottom, one to two minutes longer.

5. Transfer dough to large bowl. Cool five minutes, stirring occasionally.

6. Add one egg and, still using wooden spoon, beat until blended. Add remaining five eggs, one at a time, beating until blended after each, then beat until dough is smooth and shiny, two to three minutes.

7. Working in batches, transfer dough to pastry bag fitted with 1/2-inch plain round tip. Pipe 1 to 1-1/4-inch mounds, spaced about 2 inches apart, onto prepared baking sheets. Using wet finger, smooth tops of mounds.

8. Bake puffs fifteen minutes. Reverse baking sheets.

9 Reduce oven temperature to 350°F. Continue to bake until puffs are dry, firm, and deep golden brown, thirty to thirty-five minutes longer. Cool puffs on baking sheets.

*Go ahead and speak French. Say **Voila!***

Give Me a Lime

Lemons are fine, but nothing smells like a lime.
The green skin is divine; I love me a lime.

I'm known for my lime-glazed pound cake so fine,
there is never an un-licked tine, thanks to the lime.

The big Bundt cake takes time, which is fine
since the lime scent and taste are favorites of mine.

Ever since the first time, when people said it was sublime
The lime-glazed cream cheese pound cake has been my prime

dessert for dinnertime with friends or anytime
I need a divine dish to serve a client.

Lime-Glazed Pound Cake

Ingredients:
For the cake:
- 3-1/4 cups cake flour
- 1/4 tsp baking soda
- 1/4 tsp salt
- 2-1/4 sticks unsalted butter
- 8 ounces cream cheese
- 3 cups granulated sugar
- 6 large eggs
- 1 tsp vanilla extract
- 3 Tbsp fresh lime juice
- 2 tsp finely grated lime zest

For the glaze:
- 1/4 cup fresh lime juice
- 3/4 cup granulated sugar

Directions:
1. Ensure all ingredients are at room temperature.

2. Position a rack in the lower third of an oven and preheat to 325°F.

3. Grease and flour a 10-cup Bundt® pan; tap out excess flour.

4. To make the cake, sift together the flour, baking soda and salt; set aside.

5. In the bowl of an electric mixer fitted with the flat beater, beat the butter and cream cheese on medium speed until creamy and smooth, about thirty seconds.

6. Gradually add the granulated sugar and continue beating until light and fluffy, about five minutes, stopping the mixer occasionally to scrape down the sides of the bowl.

7. Increase the mixer speed to medium-high and add the eggs one at a time, beating well after each addition, then beat in the vanilla and lime juice.

8. Reduce the speed to low and add the flour mixture in three additions. Beat each addition just until mixed, stopping the mixer occasionally to scrape down the sides of the bowl.

9. Fold in the lime zest.

10. Spoon the batter into the prepared pan, spreading so the batter at the sides is higher than the center.

11. Bake until the cake is golden (about one hour). Start checking for doneness with a tester or toothpick at 55 mins. Some ovens may take as long as ninety mins.

12. Transfer the pan to a wire rack and let the cake cool upright in the pan for fifteen minutes.

13. Meanwhile, make the glaze: In a small bowl, whisk together the lime juice and granulated sugar until blended.

14. Set the wire rack over waxed paper, invert the pan onto the rack and lift off the pan. Poke several holes in the cake with a tester or toothpick so glaze will absorb, then brush the warm cake with the glaze. Let the cake cool completely before serving.

This cake is a winner.

Tangerine

The peel comes away in my hands,
no effort, no need for tools.
The aroma bursts forth
before the skin is pierced.

The tiny sections give up their skin
at the slightest pressure of my teeth,
the juice runs sweetness across my tongue
and down my yearning throat.

Once these were available only at Christmas,
their scent as evocative as the cedar tree
standing in front of the window,
showing off its jewelry to the neighbors.

Memories of a Christmas pageant,
being draped in white robes,
crowned with a halo, reciting
the Bible version of the birth
one month after the death of my father.

Santa came after, bearing small brown
paper bags with nuts, a few candies
and that deep orange tangerine.

This small globe of sunshine
sits in my hand, holding
then revealing, long ago memories.

Olive Oil Cake

When I read these words, I thought
deeply about olive oil. The taste,

the feel, the color appealed to me,
but in a cake? How, I wondered.

The recipe called for mandarin oranges
which grow in my neighbor's yard.

Flour, butter, sugar, vanilla, no eggs.
This could easily be vegan.

Everything sounded like a cake,
so I decided to bake one for friends.

I used vegan butter, for my vegan pals
and made this loaf pan dessert.

Fresh mandarins were a delight
to peel and squeeze for their juice.

The tang of orange lifted this cake
from what I imagined it to sublime.

Mandarin Orange Olive Oil cake
is now a regular in my repertoire.

Mandarin Orange Olive Oil Cake

Ingredients:
- 1/2 cup olive oil, plus more for the pan
- 1-1/2 cups all-purpose flour, plus more for the pan
- 1/2 tsp baking powder
- 1/4 tsp baking soda
- 1/2 tsp salt
- 3/4 cup whole milk
- 2 Tbsps unsalted butter, melted
- 1 tsp pure vanilla extract
- 1 Tbsp finely grated mandarin zest, plus 4 Ts mandarin juice (from about 6 mandarins)

Directions:
1. Pre-heat oven to 350° F.

2. Brush an 8-1/2 by 4-1/2-inch loaf pan with oil and dust with flour, tapping out the excess.

3. Whisk together the flour, baking powder, baking soda, and 1/2 tsp salt in a medium bowl; set aside.

4. In a separate bowl, whisk together the oil, milk, butter, vanilla, mandarin zest, and mandarin juice; set aside.

5. Beat the granulated sugar and eggs in a large bowl with an electric mixer on medium-high until light and fluffy, two to three minutes.

6. Reduce speed to low and add the flour mixture and the milk mixture alternately, beginning and ending with the flour mixture and mixing well between additions. (The batter will be thin.)

7. Transfer the batter to the prepared pan and bake until a toothpick inserted in the center comes out clean, sixty to seventy minutes.

8. Cool the cake in the pan for thirty minutes; transfer to a wire rack to cool completely.

This cake stays moist longer than most.

Gluten-Free Fudgy Chocolate Cake

Ingredients:
- 8-1/2 ounces (2 sticks plus 1 Tbsp) unsalted butter, plus a little more for greasing the pan
- 7 ounces bittersweet chocolate (50 percent or higher cocoa), chopped
- 5 large eggs, separated
- 1 cup sugar
- 1/2 cup almond flour
- Pinch of salt
- Whipped cream for serving (optional).

Directions:
1. Place rack in top third of oven and heat to 400°F.

2. Butter a 9-inch springform pan and set aside.

3. In a double boiler or microwave oven, melt together 8-1/2 ounces butter and the chocolate. Stir to blend.

4. In a medium bowl, stir together egg yolks and sugar. Stir in flour. Add chocolate mixture and stir until smooth.

5. Using an electric mixer, whisk egg whites and salt until stiff but not dry. Fold whites into chocolate mixture just until blended. Pour into cake pan.

6. Bake for twenty-five minutes. Remove cake from oven and allow to cool for one hour.

7. Wrap in foil and refrigerate until cake is firm and cold, at least two hours.

8. Two hours before serving, remove cake from refrigerator and bring to room temperature. Slice (center of cake will be fudgy) and serve, if desired, with whipped cream.

Your gluten-free, chocolate-loving friends will thank you.

Mom's Only Cake

Mom didn't really cook,
and rarely baked.

She could fry eggs and bacon,
make milk gravy.

Once a month she made pot roast
from pork shoulder in a crockpot.

The potatoes and carrots she added
were cooked to perfection.

She learned to bake cream puffs
and blackberry cobbler.

The cobbler was mediocre.
But she perfected one cake.

For special occasions, she got out
the cast iron skillet,

canned pineapple, maraschino cherries
brown sugar, butter, yellow cake mix.

Somehow the pineapple upside down cake
turned out exactly right, every time.

Pineapple Upside Down Cake (baked in a cast iron skillet)

Ingredients:
- 1 stick butter for the pan
- 1-1/2 cups packed brown sugar
- 1 large 20 oz. can sliced pineapple
- 1 16-20 oz. jar cherries (I prefer the ones from Trader Joe's)
- 1-1/2 cups all-purpose flour
- 2-1/2 tsps baking powder
- 1/2 tsp salt
- 1-1/2 cups white sugar
- 1/2 cup butter for the cake
- 2 eggs
- 1 cup milk
- 2 tsps pure vanilla extract

Directions

1. Preheat the oven to 375° F.

2. Melt 1 stick butter in the bottom of a cast iron skillet over medium heat, about three minutes.

3. Remove from heat and sprinkle brown sugar evenly over butter. Add pineapple slices on top of sugar in one decorative layer with a cherry in the middle of each pineapple ring. Set aside.

4. Sift flour, baking powder, and salt together in a bowl.

5. Cream sugar and butter together in a bowl. Add eggs and mix together. Add flour mixture and milk in an alternating fashion. Add vanilla extract and mix well.

5. Pour mixture evenly over pineapples in the skillet.

6. Bake until cake is golden brown, about forty minutes.

7. Let cake cool in the skillet on a rack for ten minutes before inverting onto a serving plate.

My daughter says this is literally the best recipe for Pineapple Upside Down Cake ever and she should know. She gets one every year for her birthday. This is my perfected version.

Coconut Cake, My Favorite

Whether the simple one
I can whip up in an hour,

or the advanced cake that takes
me more than half the day,

you are my favorite. Much beloved.
I relish your light sponge,

your creamy topping,
the way my heart lightens.

When I create the advanced
version, always for a special occasion,

I'm proud of what I've made.
And anxious to savor your goodness.

Coconut Cake (simple)

Ingredients:
- 2 sticks (1 cup) unsalted butter, room temperature, plus more for pan
- 2-1/2 cups all-purpose flour, plus more for pan
- 1 Tbsp baking powder
- 1/2 tsp salt
- 1-3/4 cups sugar
- 4 large eggs
- 2 tsps pure vanilla extract
- 1-1/4 cups milk
- Whipped cream (canned okay, or whip 1/2 pint of heavy cream)
- 1 cup (approx.) shredded coconut, sweetened or not

Directions for the Yellow Cake: (makes one long pan)

1. Preheat oven to 350°F. Butter one 13-inch-long pan and dust with flour, tapping out excess; set aside.

2. Into a medium bowl, sift together flours, baking powder, and salt; set aside.

3. In the bowl of an electric mixer fitted with the paddle attachment, beat the butter and sugar until light and fluffy, for three to four minutes, scraping down the sides of the bowl as needed.

4. Beat in eggs, one at a time, then beat in vanilla. With

the mixer on low speed, add the flour mixture in three parts, alternating with the milk and beginning and ending with the flour; beat until combined after each addition.

5. Pour batter into the prepared pan, and smooth with an offset spatula.

6. Bake, rotating the pan halfway through, until cake is golden brown and a cake tester inserted into the center comes out clean, thirty to thirty-five minutes.

7. Transfer pan to a wire rack to cool twenty minutes. Cake can be frosted in the pan.

Directions for Coconut Topping: (Tops one 13-inch cake)
1. Canned whipped cream is okay or whip 1/2 pint of heavy cream.
2. Spread whipped cream over cooled cake, sprinkle with coconut.

A light and easy cake to serve fresh.

Raspberry Coconut Cake (advanced)

Ingredients:
For the cake:
- 2-1/4 cups cake flour
- 3 tsps baking powder
- 1/2 tsp salt
- 8 Tbsps (1 stick) unsalted butter, softened
- 1-1/2 cups sugar
- 2 tsps finely grated lemon zest
- 1/2 tsp lemon extract
- 1-1/4 cups milk
- 1/2 cup (about 4 large) egg whites

For the frosting:
- 1/2 cup (about 4 large) egg whites
- 1 cup sugar
- 2-1/2 sticks unsalted butter, softened
- 1/4 cup strained lemon juice
- 1 tsp vanilla extract

For jam filling and coconut topping
- 1/2 cup seedless raspberry preserves
- 7-ounce bag sweetened shredded coconut

Directions for the cake:

1. Prepare two 8-inch round pans, 1-1/2 to 2 inches deep, buttered and lined with buttered parchment or wax paper.

2. Position rack in the middle of oven—preheat to 350°F.

3. Sift the cake flour, baking powder and salt onto a piece of parchment or wax paper and set aside.

4. Use an electric mixer at medium speed to beat the butter and sugar until light, about three minutes. Beat in the lemon zest and extract.

5. In a bowl, whisk together the egg whites and milk. Add a third of the flour mixture to the butter and sugar mixture and beat until smooth. Scrape down bowl and beaters.

6. Beat in half the milk and egg white mixture until incorporated, then beat in another third of the flour mixture. Scrape bowl and beaters.

7. Beat in remaining liquid until absorbed, followed by remaining flour mixture. Scrape well after each addition.

8. Divide batter between the two prepared pans and smooth top evenly. Bake in preheated oven until well risen and a toothpick inserted in the center emerges clean, about thirty to thirty-five minutes.

9. Cool layers in pans for five minutes, then invert onto racks to cool. Peel off paper.

If prepared in advance, double wrap the layers in plastic wrap and freeze or chill for up to several days in refrigerator.

Directions for Frosting:
1. To make the buttercream, combine egg whites and sugar in the bowl of an electric mixer. Whisk the contents of the bowl over a pan of simmering water until egg whites are hot and sugar is dissolved. Whip mixture by machine until cooled.

2. Switch to mixer with paddle and beat in butter until smooth.

3. Beat in lemon juice and vanilla.

To assemble cake:
1. Cut each layer into two horizontal layers, for a total of four layers.

2. Place first layer on a piece of cardboard or other stiff base, and spread with a third of the jam and a quarter of the buttercream.

3. Place another layer on top of the first and repeat (except for the cardboard!). Place another layer on and repeat again. Place the last layer on and spread the entire outside of the cake with the last quarter of the buttercream.

4. Adhere the coconut all over the outside of the cake.

5. Serve at cool room temperature. The cake can be covered lightly and refrigerated for up to two days. Bring to room temperature before serving.

My personal favorite. It's the one I make for my own birthday.

Secret Ingredient

The go-to cake in our family
is Aunt Inez's Ole Southern Butter Cake
full of butter and sugar.

You can beat it by hand, bake it
in a woodstove oven
in a battered sheet pan.

You bring it to the bereaved
on body viewing night
or funeral day.

You bring it to Memorial Day
clean up at the family cemetery.
Or baby showers, weddings,

Thanksgiving and Christmas.
When someone eats the entire cake
on body viewing night,

You go home and whip up another
for the funeral day.
The secret is your husband beats you.
You beat that into the cake.

Aunt Inez's Ole Southern Butter Cake & Sauce

<u>Ingredients</u>:
For the cake:
- 1 cup butter
- 2-3/4 cups sugar
- 5 eggs
- 1 Tbsp. vanilla
- 1 cup buttermilk
- 1/2 tsp baking soda
- 1/4 tsp salt
- 3 cups sifted flour

For the Butter Sauce:
- 1/2 cup butter
- 1/2 cup buttermilk
- 1 cup sugar
- 1 tsp vanilla

Directions for the Cake:

1. Cream the butter and sugar together.

2. Whisk the eggs in a separate dish then slowly add the eggs to the creamed mixture, beating at med-low speed just until mixed.

3. Add the buttermilk, again mixing at med-low speed.

4. Mix dry ingredients in separate bowl, and add to wet mixture in thirds, mixing at low speed after each add-in, just until blended. Do not overbeat—you are trying to maintain the air in the batter so the cake will rise properly.

5. Bake at 350°F for fifty to sixty minutes

Cool the cake on a rack for a few minutes while you prepare the Ole Southern Butter Sauce below.

Directions for the Butter Sauce:

1. Briskly boil the 1/2 cup butter, 1/2 cup buttermilk, and 1 cup sugar together for two minutes.

2. Add in the 1 tsp of vanilla and beat until cool.

3. Spread the butter sauce on the still warm cake.

If you take this to a potluck, the only thing you'll bring home is an empty baking pan.

Joy of Cheesecake

I once caused a friend
to start eating dairy again
with my New York Cheesecake.

I didn't mean to do harm
I was bringing dessert to my friends
who invited me to dinner.

Mag resisted dessert at first
until the blissful moans of her partner
broke her down.

The Joy of Cooking recipe
is not the easy no-bake kind.
It takes the finest ingredients,

and the patience of a saint.
But as my friends will testify
it is worth the time and effort.

Joy of Cooking New York Cheesecake

<u>Ingredients:</u> Preheat Oven to 350°

For the Crust:
- 2 cups graham cracker crumbs
- 1 Tbsp granulated white sugar
- 1/2 cup (one stick) melted butter

For the Cheesecake Filling:
- 1 Tbsp freshly grated lemon zest
- 1 cup granulated white sugar
- 3 Tbsps all-purpose flour
- 32 ounces cream cheese, room temperature (use full fat, not reduced or fat free cream cheese)
- 1 tsp pure vanilla extract or vanilla bean paste
- 5 large eggs, at room temperature
- 1/3 cup heavy whipping cream, room temperature

For the Topping:
- 1 cup sour cream, at room temperature (not low fat or fat free)
- 2 Tbsps granulated white sugar
- 1 tsp vanilla

Directions for the Crust:
1. In a medium sized bowl, combine the graham cracker crumbs, sugar, and melted butter and stir until all the crumbs are moistened.

2. Press the crumbs evenly over the bottom and about one inch up the sides of the springform pan.

3. Cover and refrigerate while you make the filling.

Directions for the Cheesecake Filling:

1. In a small bowl, rub the lemon zest into the sugar. Stir in the flour.

2. In bowl of your electric stand mixer, fitted with the paddle attachment (or with a hand mixer), place the cream cheese, sugar mixture, and vanilla extract. Beat on medium low speed until smooth, scraping down the sides and bottom of the bowl as needed.

3. Add the eggs, one at a time, beating well (about thirty seconds) after each addition.

4. Add the whipping cream and beat until incorporated.

5. Remove the crust from the refrigerator and pour in the filling.

6. Place the springform pan on a larger baking pan, to catch any drips, and place in the oven.

7. Bake for fifteen minutes and then lower the oven temperature to 250 degrees F and continue to bake for about another sixty to seventy minutes or until firm (the center of the cheesecake will still look a little wet, and if you gently shake the pan the cheesecake will jiggle just a bit).

8. Remove from oven and place on a wire rack.

Directions for the Topping:

1. In a small bowl combine the sour cream, sugar, and vanilla extract.

2. Spread the topping over the warm cheesecake and return to oven to bake for about fifteen minutes.

3. Remove from oven and place on a wire rack. Immediately run a knife or spatula around the inside edge of pan to loosen the cheesecake (helps prevent the surface from cracking as it cools).

4. Let cool completely at room temperature and then place in the refrigerator, uncovered, to chill for about one hour.

5. Then cover with plastic wrap and chill for at least eight hours, preferably overnight.

*Cheesecake is one of those bakes
I never regret making.*

Outro

When the Cupboard Contains Only Onions and Olive Oil

Onions are like people
When oiled, they are easy to peel.
If expecting high heat, use olive oil.

Cover your body in onion skins.
Anoint your head with oil.
Be like water and flow.

If onions make you cry, you're only human.
Humans, if well-oiled, may cry.

Swallow your tears to tame onion breath.
Wallow in oil, even though your body
is made of water.

Afterword

I didn't grow up cooking and baking. In fact when I got married at age fifteen I knew how to cook only boxed mac and cheese, mashed potatoes, and fried meat. After I came out and attended multiple lesbian potluck dinners where the array of homemade entrees, salads, and desserts was eye-opening, I took cooking and baking seriously. I was already a vegetarian, and I learned how to make quick and easy meals.

Later, I began to bake with intention. I became allergic to corn and corn products, so if I wanted dessert, I had to make my own. I made beautiful fruit plates coated with sugar for holidays. I baked cakes and decorated with sugared edible flowers. I experimented with every dessert recipe that tempted my taste buds.

Potluck dinners with homemade food and desserts may be a thing of the past, or maybe of the future, but cooking and baking for yourself and your loved ones is rewarding and something a person can do regularly. We have to eat; we may as well eat well.

Sandra de Helen
Portland, Oregon
June 2022

About The Author

Sandra de Helen lives and writes in Portland, Oregon. She is author of the Shirley Combs/Dr. Mary Watson mystery series, set in Portland; *Till Darkness Comes*, a thriller set in Kansas City, Missouri; and (now) five collections of lesbian poetry published by Launch Point Press.

See more of her work at **www.SandradeHelen.com**.

Sandra is a member of the Golden Crown Literary Society, Dramatists Guild, Honor Roll!, and the International Centre for Women Playwrights.

Follow her on **Instagram @dehelen**
And like her on **Facebook** at:
https://www.facebook.com/SandradeHelenAuthor/

Acknowledgments

I appreciate everyone who contributed to my ability to cook and bake. My daughter started cooking and baking when she was eight years old. I learned from her to add spices and to venture beyond the usual foods. I learned to try food and recipes from other countries.

The Good Housekeeping Cookbook of 1957 taught me how to shop for ingredients, how to use cooking utensils, how to read recipes, and how to properly set a table. *The Joy of Cooking* remains a favorite cookbook for its wide variety of desserts. *The Moosewood Cookbook* showed me that vegetarian food could be rich and delicious. And Julia Child's *Mastering the Art of French Cooking* showed me I didn't have to be afraid to make a soufflé.

I thank my sister for preserving and sharing our Aunt Inez's handwritten recipe for Ole Southern Butter Cake. My mom wrote out her recipe for Cream Puffs. Grandma Maggie (my mom's mom) taught me to make pie crust. She never measured anything, but she showed me with her own hands what to do. I call on her spirit to help me every time I attempt anything with dough.

Cooking/Baking Conversion Charts

Oven Temperatures Fahrenheit to Celsius
- 250 F = 120 c
- 320 F = 160 c
- 350 F = 180 c
- 400 F = 205 c
- 425 F = 220 c

Volume
- 1/4 teaspoon = 1 milliliter (ml)
- 1 teaspoon (tsp) = 5ml
- 1 tablespoon (tbsp.) = 15 ml
- 1 cup or 8 fluid ounces = 240 ml
- 34 fluid ounces = 1 liter

Conversions to Metric Measurements
- 1/2 tsp = 2.5 ml
- 1 tsp = 5 ml
- 1 tbsp = 15 ml
- 1 fluid ounce = 30 ml
- 1 cup = 237 ml
- 1 pint (2 cups) = 473 ml
- 1 quart (4 cups) = .95 liter
- 1 gallon (16 cups) = 3.8 liters
- 1 ounce (oz.) = 28 grams
- 1 pound = 454 grams

What Pans Will Hold (2-inch/5 cm deep)

Round Pans
6×2 inches (15 x 5cm) = 4 cups (960ml)
8×2 inches (20 x 5cm) = 6 cups (1.4 liters)
9×2 inches (23 x 5cm) = 8 cups (1.9 liters)

Square Pans
8×2 inch (20 x 5 cm) = 8 cups (1.9 liters)
9×2 inch (23 x 5 cm) = 10 cups (2.4 liters)
10×2 inch = (25 x 5 cm) = 12 cups (2.8 liters)

Rectangular Pans
11×7 inches (28 x 18 cm) = 10 cups (2.4 liters)
13×9 inches (33 x 23 cm) = 14 cups (3.3 liters)

Loaf Pans
(about 3 inches/8 cm) tall)
8×4 inch (20 x 10 cm) = 4 cups (960 ml)
9×5 inch (23 x 13 cm) = 8 cups (1.9 liters)

Baking in grams
- 1 cup flour = 140 grams
- 1 cup sugar = 150 grams
- 1 cup heavy cream = 235 grams

Weight
- .035 ounces = 1 gram
- 3.5 ounces = 100 grams
- 1.1 pounds = 500 grams

Cup Conversions

- 1 cup = 8 fluid ounces
- 1 cup = 16 tablespoons
- 1 cup = 48 teaspoons
- 1 cup = 1/2 pint
- 1 cup = 1/4 quart
- 1 cup = 1/16 gallon
- 1 cup = 240 ml

www.ingramcontent.com/pod-product-compliance
Lightning Source LLC
Chambersburg PA
CBHW070110080526
44586CB00013B/1254